CW00349831

Other 'crazy' gigglebooks by Bill Stott
Football – it drives us crazy!
Marriage – it drives us crazy!
Cats – they drive us crazy!
Computers – they drive us crazy!
Golf – it drives us crazy!

Published in 2007 by Helen Exley Giftbooks in Great Britain

12 11 10 9 8 7 6 5 4 3 2 1

Selection and arrangement copyright © 2007 Helen Exley
Cartoons copyright © 2007 Bill Stott

ISBN 13: 978-1-84634-201-1

Edited by Gayle Morgan
Series Editor: Helen Exley

Printed in China

Helen Exley Giftbooks, 16 Chalk Hill, Watford, Herts, WD19 4BG, UK
www.helenexleygiftbooks.com

Middle Age

IT DRIVES US CRAZY!

CARTOONS BY
BILL STOTT

BEEN THERE
DONE IT ALL
AND
UP FOR MORE!

A HELEN EXLEY
GIGGLEBOOK

"There's no way he would've done that at your age Son."

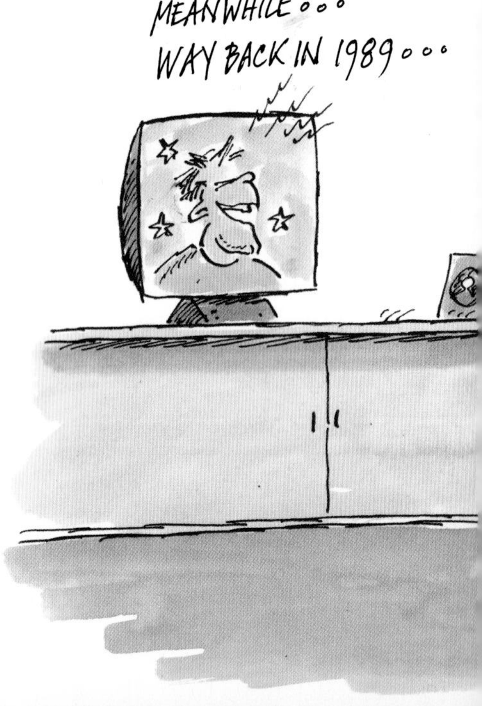
MEANWHILE ...
WAY BACK IN 1989 ...

"I just feel we're slipping
into middle age. We need
to kick-start our lives.
Know what I mean?"

"My Dad's really embarrassing.
He's seriously old – like at least 40
and he pretends he likes **my** music!"

"Wow Dad!
In dog years,
you'd be 350!"

"When I was 20, getting ready to go out took no time. Now I'm in my 40s, it takes two hours. If I ever get to 80, it won't be worth going out."

"You have to be impressed. He's 40 today and he can still get into his flares."

"Wig, wig, facelift, tummy tuck, wig, facelift, wig, boob job, wig...."

"50's been a real watershed for Gavin. After years of conformity, decades of being Mr Average, he's finally gone and done it, and...."

"He's wearing his shirt outside his trousers!"

"Receeding hairline? Nonsense –
I've always combed my hair forward."

"You found a wrinkle? Give it 25 years and you won't have to look for them."

"OK. As of now, I'm moving into elegant and languid mode...."

"Well yes –
flares are back
in. But hair
pieces aren't."

"And you two looked like that on purpose! Weird!"

"Well, that seventh lift's certainly got rid of the bags and wrinkles."

"Whose is this work of fiction?"

"Don't worry about it – it happens quite often on our second honeymoon breaks...."

"Well yes, I can imagine
my parents doing it.
But not together."

"Alan's at his best right now. He was born middle-aged."

"You know what they say about being as old as you feel? I think I'm about 328."

"Honey – come quick –
I've found a brown hair!"

"He's still upset. He got the nose stud, the earring, the tattoo, shaved his head. ...And still looks middle-aged."

"Wow, retro-dancing! I love it."

"It's not natural –
a ten year old in a
forty eight year
old body...."

"I wonder what you'd look like
without your chins?"

"HMMM."

"And I just love history – My Dad often tells me stories about the olden days, way back in the 80s."

"It is not a white hair.
It is a distinguished silver hair!"

"He bet his allowance that he could do more press-ups than Grandad. He lost."

"Why don't you do something useful
instead of striding about pretending you
haven't got a double chin?"

"Don't get me wrong – a mountain bike
is youthful – personally though – I'd lose
the lycra pants...."

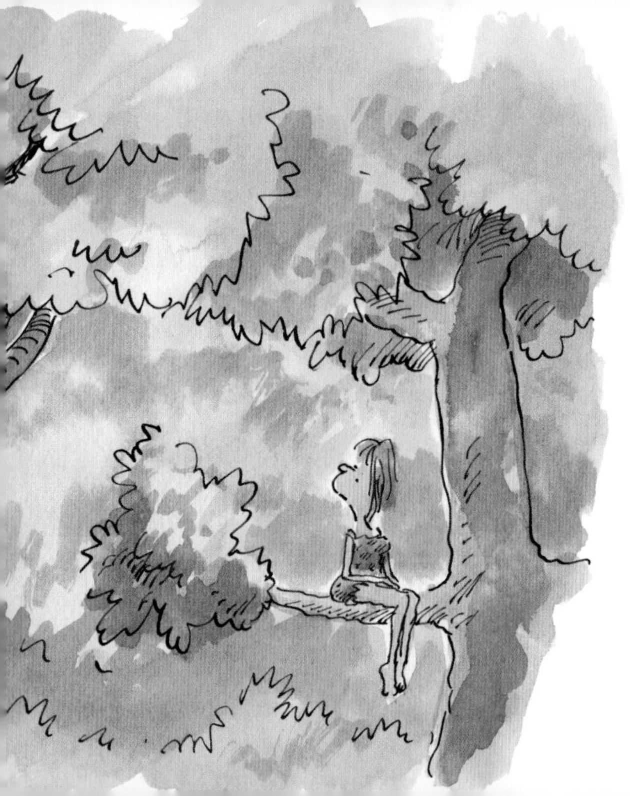

"Memories are OK – I just wish they
didn't go back so far...."

"Trust me. That lost youth of ours is just
over the next rise...."

"Life is out there for the taking Son.
When I was your age I thought a ride-on
mower was just a crazy dream...."

"Now that's what a grandma should look like, Grandma."

About Bill Stott

Bill Stott is a freelance cartoonist whose work never fails to pinpoint the absurd and simply daft moments in our daily lives. Originally Head of Arts faculty at a city high school, Bill launched himself as a freelance cartoonist. With sales of over 2.8 million books with Helen Exley Giftbooks, Bill has an impressive portfolio of 34 published titles, including his very successful *Spread of Over 40s' Jokes* and *Triumph of Over 50s' Jokes*.

Bill's work appears in many publications and magazines, ranging from the *The Times Educational Supplement* to *Practical Poultry*. An acclaimed after-dinner speaker, Bill subjects his audience to a generous helping of his wit and wisdom, illustrated with cartoons drawn deftly on the spot!

What is a Helen Exley giftbook?

We hope you enjoy *Middle Age – it drives us crazy!* It's just one of many hilarious cartoon books available from Helen Exley Giftbooks, all of which make special gifts. We try our best to bring you the funniest jokes because we want every book we publish to be great to give, great to receive.

HELEN EXLEY GIFTBOOKS creates gifts for all special occasions – not just birthdays, anniversaries and weddings, but for those times when you just want to say 'thanks' or make someone laugh. Why not visit our website, www. helenexleygiftbooks.com, and browse through all our gift ideas?

ALSO BY BILL STOTT
Marriage – it drives us crazy!
Cats – they drive us crazy!
Football – it drives us crazy!
Sex – it drives us crazy!
Golf – it drives us crazy!

Information on all our titles is also available from:
Helen Exley Giftbooks, 16 Chalk Hill, Watford WD19 4BG, UK.
www.helenexleygiftbooks.com